Bread Machine Recipe

By Brad Hoskinson

Copyright 2022 by Brad Hoskinson. All rights reserved.

No part of this book may be reproduced in any form or by any electronic or mechanical means, including information storage and retrieval systems, without written permission from the author, except for the use of brief quotations in a book review.

Table of Contents

Bread Machine Hot Cross Buns 5

Bread Machine Apple Bread with Nuts 7

Bread Machine - Banana Bread Recipe (Classic Version) 9

Bread Machine - Bacon Bread 11

Bread Machine Breadsticks (Soft & Chewy) 13

Bread Machine - Butter Bread Recipe 15

Bread Machine Buttermilk Bread (Soft White Bread) 17

Buttermilk Bread Recipe (Soft White Bread) 19

Bread Machine - Cake Bread 22

Bread Machine Calzone Dough 24

Bread Machine – Cheese Bread 26

Bread Machine Chocolate Cake 28

Bread Machine - Chocolate Chip Bread 30

Bread Machine Cinnamon Bread (Chocolate Chip) 32

Bread Machine Cinnamon Raisin Bread (Golden Raisins) 34

Bread Machine Cornbread – Sweet & Buttery 36

All Purpose Flour Bread Machine Recipe (Country White Bread) 38

Bread Machine Cranberry Bread (with Walnuts) 40

Cranberry Walnut Bread 42

Bread Machine Cranberry Raisin Bread 46

Flaxseed Bread Recipe (Sandwich Bread) 48

Bread Machine French Bread – Easy Baguette Recipe 52

Bread Machine Garlic Bread 54

Bread Machine Gingerbread 56

Greek Yogurt Bread (Soft & Fluffy White Bread) 58

Bread Machine Honey Wheat Bread 62

Bread Machine Italian Bread 64

Bread Machine – Italian Herb Bread 66
Bread Machine - Jalapeno Cheese Bread... 68
Bread Machine Jalapeno Cornbread (with Cheese).................................. 70

Bread Machine Hot Cross Buns

Although hot cross buns are typically associated with Easter, these spiced buns can be enjoyed year-round. The sweet, rich flavor of the buns is a perfect complement to any meal. And what could be more convenient than making them in a bread machine? This recipe for bread machine hot cross buns is easy to follow and yields delicious results.

Prep Time 20 mins | Cook Time 25 mins | Total Time 1 hrs 45 mins

Ingredients

- 3/4 cup lukewarm milk (low-fat is fine)
- 2 1/2 teaspoons pure vanilla extract
- 1 large egg, at room temperature
- 3 1/2 cups all-purpose flour
- 1/3 cup granulated sugar
- 1 scant teaspoon salt
- 2 1/2 teaspoons active dry yeast
- 2 ounces (1/4 cup) unsalted butter, softened, cut into 4 to 6 pieces
- 1 1/2 teaspoons ground cinnamon
- 3/4 to 1 cup currants
- 1 large egg yolk
- 2 1/2 tablespoons of water

For the Icing:

- 1 cups confectioners' sugar
- 2 1/2 tablespoons milk
- 1 teaspoon pure vanilla extract

Instructions

1. Gather the ingredients.
2. Whisk together the 3/4 cup milk, 2 1/2 teaspoons of vanilla, and the egg.
3. Churn the milk, white flour, brown sugar, salt, yeast, and butter into the bread machine, using the brewing order made by your bread machine manufacturer.

4. Set the machine on the dough cycle; add cinnamon, currants, or chopped dried fruit at the beep. If the mixture seems too dry, add water in very small amounts.
5. When the dough is done and doubled in volume, remove to a lightly floured surface. Punch down, knead about 6 to 8 times, and let it rest for 10-15 minutes.
6. Grease a 9-inch square baking pan.
7. Form small pieces of dough (about 2 to 2 1/4 ounces each) into balls and place the dough balls in the pre-heated baking pan. Cover the pan with a cloth and leave the dough to rise in a moderate environment for about 40 minutes.
8. Preheat the oven to 350 F. Stir the egg yolk and 2 tablespoons of water. Lightly brush the tops of the buns with the egg yolk mixture. Bake for 22-25 minutes until the tops are nicely browned. Remove the pan to a rack to cool completely.
9. Dissolve confectioners' sugar into milk, then add 2 tablespoons of vanilla and 1 2 teaspoons sugar; stir until smooth. Add liquid gradually while the confectioners' sugar is in the process of becoming lumpy and stiff, and stir constantly to obtain drizzling consistency.
10. With a spoon or decorating bag, drizzle crosses on the tops of the buns.! Let the bread cool on the cooling rack for 1 to 2 hours.

Bread Machine Apple Bread with Nuts

Apple bread is a type of quick bread made with apples. It is a sweet bread that can be made in a bread machine. Apple bread can be made with or without nuts. This recipe for apple bread with nuts is an excellent way to use apples that are starting to go bad. The bread can be served plain or with butter.

Prep Time 10 mins | Cook Time 1 hr 40 mins | Total Time 1 hr 50 mins

Ingredients

- ✓ 2 Cups Applesauce (chunky-style) - 250 milliliters
- ✓ 3/4 Cup Vegetable Oil (use a neutral flavored oil such as canola oil) - 59 milliliters
- ✓ 4 Eggs
- ✓ 3 Cups Flour (all-purpose flour) - 250 grams
- ✓ 1 Cup White Granulated Sugar - 150 grams
- ✓ 1 Cup Light Brown Sugar (packed cup) - 117 grams
- ✓ 2 Teaspoons Vanilla Extract - 10 milliliters
- ✓ 2 Teaspoons Baking Powder - 10 milliliters
- ✓ 2 Teaspoons Baking Soda - 10 milliliters
- ✓ 1 Teaspoon Ground Cinnamon – 3.5 milliliters
- ✓ 1 Teaspoon salt – 3.5 milliliters
- ✓ 2 Cups Chopped Walnuts - 135 grams

Instructions

1. Unplug the bread machine and remove the bread pan.
2. Lightly beat the eggs.
3. Add the applesauce, vegetable oil, eggs, and other ingredients (except the chopped walnuts) into the bread pan.
4. Place the pan back into the bread machine and then plug in the bread machine.
5. Enter the correct bread machine settings (Sweet Quick Bread, Light Color, 2 lb) and press the start button.
6. Wait until the closing mixing cycle until the chopped onions have been added.

7. Unplug your bread machine when the bread machine has finished baking the quick bread. Remove the bread pan and place it on a wooden cutting board. Leave the bread in the pan for 10 minutes before you remove it from the bread pan. Protect your hands with oven mitts when removing the bread pan because you will work with it while it is hot.
8. When removing the quick bread from its bread pan, put it on a cooling rack in the oven. When using the baking implements, be sure to use oven mitts. Let the quick bread fry for 62 minutes at 200 degrees Fahrenheit, or it becomes increasingly prone to breaking when it is sliced.
9. Don't forget to remove the mixing paddle if it is stuck in the bread. Use oven mitts as the mixing paddle could be hot.

Bread Machine - Banana Bread Recipe
(Classic Version)

Banana bread is a classic recipe that can be made in a bread machine. This version of the recipe is a classic, with a few simple ingredients. The bread machine makes it easy to make banana bread, and the results are delicious. This recipe is perfect for anyone who loves banana bread.

Prep Time 15 mins | Cook Time 1 hr 45 mins | Total Time 2 hr

Ingredients

- ✓ 10 Tablespoons Unsalted Butter (softened)
- ✓ 3 Eggs (lightly beaten)
- ✓ 2 Teaspoons Vanilla Extract
- ✓ 4 Bananas (ripe & medium-sized bananas) - 4 medium bananas equal roughly 1 cup of mashed bananas.
- ✓ 2 Cup Light Brown Sugar (packed cup)
- ✓ 3 Cups Flour (all-purpose)
- ✓ 1 Teaspoon Salt
- ✓ 2 Teaspoons Baking Powder (aluminum free)
- ✓ 2 Teaspoons Baking Soda
- ✓ 1 Cup Chopped Walnuts or MINI Chocolate Chips (optional)

Instructions

1. Bread Machine Settings – Sweet Quick Bread, Light Color, 3 lb
2. Beat the eggs.
3. Mash bananas with a fork.
4. Soften the butter in the microwave.
5. Start by putting in the butter, eggs, and bananas, among other ingredients. Suppose you follow a pre-arranged order as described in the following mix-ins. In that case, liquids should be mixed with the dry ingredients first and the dry ingredients second, placing them in the first compartment of the bread machine. This helps to avoid spilling any material inside the bread machine. The bread machine should always be unplugged when removing the bread pan.

6. Put the bread pan (with all ingredients) back into the bread machine, close the lid, and then plug in the bread machine.
7. Enter the bread machine settings (Sweet Quick Bread, Light Color) and press the start button.
8. Optional - If you're considering adding chopped walnuts or miniature chocolate chips to enhance this basic banana bread recipe, you can add them after the first bread machine mixing cycle and before the second mixing (final mixing).
9. When the bread-maker has completed baking, unplug the machine, take the bread pan off the cooking platform, and set it down onto a sharp cutting board. Wear oven mitts while unplugging the bread maker since it is quite hot!
10. Optional - Use a long wooden skewer to test if the banana bread is thoroughly cooked. Wear oven mitts as the bread pan will be hot. See the tips section for more details on this classic "toothpick" test.
11. You need to let banana bread stay in the oven's warm bread pan for ten minutes (as this finishes the baking process) if you use a mechanical bread machine before removing the banana bread from the bread pan. Do not retrieve hot items with bare hands, and wear oven mitts.
12. After 10 minutes of "cool down," you should remove the banana bread from the bread pan and place the banana bread on a wire cooling rack to finish cooling. Use oven mitts when removing the bread.
13. Don't forget to remove the mixing paddle if it is stuck in the bread. Use oven mitts as the mixing paddle could be hot.
14. You should allow the bread to enable fully cool before the angel food cake is cut itself. This can take up up to two hours to complete. Otherwise, the angel food cake will crumble (crumble) more easily when cut.

Bread Machine - Bacon Bread

Bacon bread is a delicious and easy-to-make treat that can be enjoyed anytime. With just a few simple ingredients, you can have fresh, warm bacon bread in no time. Whether you're looking for a savory breakfast option or a tasty snack, this recipe is sure to please. So, fire up your bread machine and enjoy the best bacon bread you've ever had!

Prep Time 7 mins | Cook Time 3.30 hrs | Total Time 3 hrs 37 mins

Ingredients

- ✓ 2 Cups - Water (warm)
- ✓ 5 Tablespoons - Butter (sliced)
- ✓ 4 Cups - Bread Flour
- ✓ 2 Cups - One Minute Oatmeal
- ✓ 2 Teaspoons - Salt
- ✓ 3/4 Cup - Dark Brown Sugar
- ✓ 2 Teaspoons - Bread Machine Yeast
- ✓ 5 Tablespoons - Bacon Bits

Instructions

1. Bread Machine settings – 3-pound loaf, light color, and "basic" bread setting.
2. Unplug the bread machine and remove the bread pan.
3. Add all ingredients (except the bacon bits), starting with the water, into the bread machine "bucket" (loaf pan). Place the bread machine yeast in last and the yeast should not touch the water (until the bread machine is turned on and the ingredients start to be mixed together).
4. Place the bread pan back into the bread machine and plug in the bread machine.
5. Enter the correct settings (2lb, light color and basic) and press the "start" button.
6. After the bread machine has finished its FIRST kneading cycle, add the bacon bits. You can add them with the other ingredients, but the bacon bits will be more broken up and very small if they go through two kneading cycles. Wear oven mitts.

7. After the bread machine has finished its FINAL kneading cycle and before the baking process starts, gently sprinkle some bacon bits on top of the dough. Wear oven mitts.
8. Go to the cooling rack once the bread has finished baking in the bread machine. Use oven mitts when lifting the container out of the bread machine, as it will be very hot!
9. In our Sunbeam bread machine, a 3-pound loaf takes between 3.30 and three hours to bake at a light and basic bread setting. However, the time in various bread machines can differ, so it is best to check your bread machine before the alarm "Ended"! Your bread-maker is programmed to exhibit the duration of a baked good the moment you set the time settings. This will teach you when to go to the kitchen to obtain the bread.

Bread Machine Breadsticks (Soft & Chewy)

If you're looking for a quick and easy way to make soft and chewy breadsticks, look no further than your trusty bread machine. With just a few simple ingredients, you can have delicious breadsticks on the table in no time. Best of all, they're sure to please even the pickiest of eaters.

Prep Time 1 hr 45 mins | Cook Time 15 mins | Total Time 2 hr

Ingredients

- ✓ 2 Cups Water (lukewarm)
- ✓ 3 Tablespoons Olive Oil
- ✓ 4 Cups Flour (all-purpose flour or bread flour)
- ✓ 2 Tablespoons White Granulated Sugar
- ✓ 2 Teaspoons Italian Herb Seasoning (optional)
- ✓ 2 Teaspoons Salt
- ✓ 3 Teaspoons Bread Machine Yeast
- ✓ 2 Teaspoons Large Crystal Salt (to sprinkle on top of the breadsticks before baking)

Instructions

1. Place the water, olive oil, and other ingredients into the bread pan. You can make a little indent on the top of the flour to avoid the yeast falling into the water (until the machine starts). Do not combine the salt with the yeast (as the salt can kill the yeast). Place the yeast & salt in separate parts of the bread pan.
2. Place the butter pan (with ingredients) into your unplugged bread machine and then plug the machine in.
3. On the Dough setting, place your bread machine on the bed and press the start button. In our Sunbeam bread machine, the kneading and rising process take at least one and a half hours.
4. When your bread machine has finished, unplug the machine & pour the dough onto a cutting board. Wear oven mitts when handling the bread pan, as it may be hot. However, sprinkle some flour on the cutting board (before you pour the dough) to help prevent the dough from sticking to the cutting board.
5. Preheat the oven to 450 degrees F.

6. Shape the breadstick dough by cutting it into thin strips or rolling it into thin tubes. See the tips section below for more information on how to shape your breadsticks.
7. Transfer the dough breadsticks to a nonstick baking sheet. Cover the dough using plastic wrap, a thin wet towel, and so forth. Do not let the dough dry out or gather dust. Let it rise for 30 minutes on the baking sheet. The dough should nearly double in width during this time.
8. Place the dough breadsticks on parchment paper unlined with a baking sheet. Use a small pastry brush to coat the dough breadsticks with a thin layer of olive oil. Then top each dough breadstick with a large salt crystal (i.e., sea salt or coarse kosher salt).
9. Place the baking sheet in the oven for 15-17 minutes.
10. Remove from the oven when finished and let the breadsticks cool for 2 or 3 minutes on a cooling rack.
11. For best results, serve & eat while the breadsticks are still slightly warm.

Bread Machine - Butter Bread Recipe

If you're looking for a delicious and easy bread recipe at home, look no further than this butter bread recipe made in a bread machine. This recipe is foolproof and yields a beautifully soft and fluffy loaf of bread perfect for toast, sandwiches, or even just eating plain. Best of all, it only takes a few minutes of hands-on time and the bread machine does all the work for you.

Prep Time 10 mins | Cook Time 3.30 hrs | Total Time 3 hrs 40 mins

Ingredients

- ✓ 2 Cups - Milk (lukewarm)
- ✓ 10 Tablespoons - Butter (sliced)
- ✓ 5 Cups - Bread Flour
- ✓ 2 Cups - Oatmeal (one-minute oatmeal)
- ✓ 3 Tablespoons - Sugar (white granulated)
- ✓ 2 Teaspoons - Salt
- ✓ 2 Teaspoons - Bread Machine Yeast

Instructions

1. Bread Machine settings – 3-pound loaf, light color, and "basic" bread setting.
2. Unplug the bread machine & remove the bread pan.
3. Add all ingredients starting with the milk, into the bread machine "bucket" (bread pan). Then place the bread pan into the bread machine.
4. Plug in the bread machine. Enter the correct settings (3 lb, light color & basic bread) and press the "start" button.
5. As soon as the bread machine has completed its baking process, disconnect the bread machine from the power outlet. Remove the bread pan from the inside of the bread machine. Then remove the bread from the loaf pan and place it on a plate. Use oven mitts when removing the bread maker container (bread loaf pan) to avoid burning your hands.
6. After removing the bread, don't forget to remove the mixing paddle if it is stuck in the bread. Use oven mitts as the mixing paddle will

be very hot from the bread machine. Or wait until the bread is thoroughly cooled and then remove the mixing paddle.
7. In our Sunbeam bread machine, it takes about 3 hours to complete a 2-pound batch of bread in the Light color & basic bread settings. However, some machines may have different lengths for baking and you won't be home when the bread maker "finished" alarm sounds! Your bread machine should show you the length of the baking time after you have entered the settings into the machine. This will allow you to know when to be in the kitchen to remove the bread.
8. Before using your bread machine, you should read the manufacturer's instructions to use the bread machine effectively and safely.

Bread Machine Buttermilk Bread (Soft White Bread)

If you don't have buttermilk on hand, no worries! You can easily make it with milk and lemon juice or vinegar. This bread machine buttermilk bread (soft white bread) recipe is perfect for beginners. Just add the ingredients to your bread machine pan in the order listed and let the machine do the work.

Prep Time 15 mins | Cook Time 2 hrs 55 mins | Total Time 3 hrs 10 mins

Ingredients

Ingredients – Bread Machine Buttermilk Bread – 2 lb Setting

- ✓ 2 Cups Buttermilk (lukewarm) – 285 grams
- ✓ 3 Tablespoons Unsalted Butter (softened) – 29 grams
- ✓ 4 Cups Bread Flour – 360 grams
- ✓ 2 Tablespoons White Granulated Sugar – 19 grams
- ✓ 2 Teaspoons salt – 5 milliliters
- ✓ 2 Teaspoons Instant Yeast (Bread Machine Yeast) – 5 milliliters – Not active dry yeast

Ingredients – Bread Machine Buttermilk Bread – 2 lb Setting

- ✓ 2 Cups Buttermilk (lukewarm) – 307 milliliters
- ✓ 5 Tablespoons Unsalted Butter (softened) – 57 grams
- ✓ 4 Cups Bread Flour – 420 grams
- ✓ 2 Tablespoons White Granulated Sugar – 19 grams
- ✓ 2 Teaspoons Salt – 6 milliliters
- ✓ 2 Teaspoons Instant Yeast (Bread Machine Yeast) – 7 milliliters – Not active dry yeast

Instructions

1. Settings – 2 lb loaf (2 lb, light color and basic bread) and 3 lb loaf (3 lb, golden color and basic bread)
2. Unplug your bread machine.

3. Remove the bread pan from the bread machine (so when you add the ingredients, they can not accidentally spill into the machine).
4. Soften the butter in your microwave.
5. Add the cold milk to the bread pan and place all other ingredients into it except for the bread machine yeast. Then turn the bread machine on and wait until all of the ingredients have been mixed by the bread machine. Place the bread pan back inside the bread machine and cover with a lid or plastic wrap to lock in the steam and prevent the yeast from activating.
6. Plug in the bread machine. Enter the correct settings (2 lb or 3lb, light color & basic bread) and press the "start" button.
7. When the bread machine has finished baking the bread, unplug the bread machine.
8. Take the bread pan out of the bread machine.
9. Place the bread on the rack and then remove it from the bread maker. Wear oven mitts when scraping the bread from the bread maker, as it will be very hot! Allow the bread to cool down on the rack for at least one hour.
10. After removing the bread, don't forget to remove the mixing paddle if it is stuck in the bread. Use oven mitts as the mixing paddle will be very hot from the bread machine. Or wait until the bread is thoroughly cooled and then remove the mixing paddle.

Buttermilk Bread Recipe (Soft White Bread)

This bread recipe is one of my favorites! It's so easy to make and the result is a soft, white loaf of bread that's perfect for any occasion. The best part about this recipe is that it only requires a few simple ingredients you probably already have in your kitchen. So, if you're looking for an easy and delicious bread recipe, give this one a try!

> Prep Time 2 hrs 50 mins | Cook Time 45 mins | Total Time 3 hrs 35 mins

Ingredients

- ✓ 2 Cups Buttermilk (warm) – 327 milliliters
- ✓ 5 Tablespoons Unsalted Butter (softened) – 67 grams
- ✓ 4 Cups Bread Flour – 430 grams
- ✓ 2 Tablespoons White Granulated Sugar – 29 grams
- ✓ 2 Teaspoons salt – 9.5 milliliters
- ✓ 2 Teaspoons Instant Yeast – 9.5 milliliters

Instructions

Creating Dough with a Bread Machine

1. Unplug your bread machine.
2. Remove the bread pan from the bread machine.
3. Add the buttermilk to the bread pan, then add the other ingredients. Pour the instant yeast last, and let this yeast not touch the liquid (until the bread machine is turned on and mixing the ingredients above). Some bakers like to make a small indent on the top of the flour to prevent the yeast from spilling into the liquids or mixing with the salt before the machine is turned on.
4. Put the bread pan with ingredients back into the unplugged bread machine.
5. Plug in the bread machine. Enter the "Dough" setting on your bread machine and press the "Start" button.
6. When the bread machine has finished making the bread dough, unplug the bread machine.
7. Remove the bread pan (with the dough) from the bread machine.

8. Now go to the instruction section below: "preparing the dough & baking the bread." FYI – Ignore the electric stand mixer below instructions if you use a bread machine to make your dough. Skip down to the preparing the dough & baking the bread section down.

Creating Dough with an Electric Stand Mixer with Dough Hook

1. Unplug your electric stand mixer.
2. Remove the mixing bowl from the electric mixer.
3. Insert the dough hook into the electric mixer.
4. First, pour the buttermilk into the mixing bowl and include the other baking powder and yeast. Place the yeast in the bowl and skip one until mixing is completed (the instant yeast should not touch the liquid, so there is no issue). Some bakers like to make a small indent on the top of the flour to prevent the yeast from spilling into the liquids or mixing with the salt before the machine is turned on.
5. Place the mixing bowl back into the electric stand mixer.
6. Plug in the electric mixer and use a low speed (i.e., setting 2) to mix the dough. Mix & knead the dough for 9-13 minutes.
7. Turn off the electric mixer and unplug the machine.
8. Remove the mixing bowl from the electric mixer. Pour the dough into a second large mixing bowl lightly "greased" with olive oil, melted butter, cooking spray, etc.
9. Optional – Lightly coat the top of the dough with vegetable oil to prevent the dough exterior from drying out.
10. Loosely cover the bowl with plastic wrap and let the dough rise for 65-95 minutes until it doubles roughly in size. See tips below for more information.
11. After the dough has risen, go to the instruction section below on "preparing the dough & baking the bread."

Preparing the Dough & Baking the Bread

1. Sprinkle a little bit of flour onto a large cutting board.
2. Remove the dough from the bread pan or mixing bowl and place the dough on the cutting board.

3. Press down on the dough with your hands and create a "flattish" rectangle with the dough. The dough should be roughly 1 inch high.
4. Roll up the dough into a tight "jelly roll."
5. Place the rolled-up dough into the bread pan.
6. Apply soft pressure with your fingertips on the top of the bread dough, so the edges of the dough press down, forcing the gaps between the dough and the bread pan to close. This helps the bread turn into an excellent loaf shape without missing edges. Make sure that the top of the pressed-down dough is roughly level (so one side isn't much higher than the other).
7. Optional – Lightly coat the top of the dough with vegetable oil to prevent the dough exterior from drying out.
8. Loosely cover the entire top of the bread pan with plastic wrap. Set the covered bread pan aside for 50-65 minutes for the dough to rise into a loaf shape. When the dough has risen modestly (1 2 cm to 1 inch) over the top of the bread pan, it's time to place the bread pan in the oven. FYI, do not wait for the dough to rise higher (or the bread top will be too large after baking). The dough's rising process will continue in the oven.
9. During this "rising" period, preheat the oven to 370 F. This should be done at least 15-20 minutes before you expect to put the dough & bread pan into the oven.
10. Place the bread pan in the (preheated) oven to bake at 370 F for 40-47 minutes. Wear oven mitts when dealing with a hot oven. Place the bread pan in the middle of the oven.
11. Rotate the bread pan in the oven after 20-25 minutes (to ensure even browning of the bread).
12. After the 40-45 minute baking period, remove the bread pan from the oven. Wear oven mitts.
13. Remove the bread from the bread pan and place the bread on a wire cooling rack. Wear oven mitts.
14. Optional – Brush melted butter on the bread with a pastry brush. This "basting" helps to create a more golden & tasty crust.
15. Allow the bread to cool down on the wire cooling rack for 1-2 hours before cutting the bread.

Bread Machine - Cake Bread

Baking bread is a process that takes time and patience. But with a bread machine, you can have freshly baked bread without all the hassle. Cake bread is a type of bread that is made with a sweeter batter, similar to that of a cake. It's perfect for those who want cake taste but in bread form.

Prep Time 10 mins | Cook Time 3.10 hrs | Total Time 3 hrs 20 mins

Ingredients

- ✓ 2 Cups Water (warm)
- ✓ 5 Tablespoons Unsalted Butter (sliced)
- ✓ 4 Cups Bread Flour
- ✓ 2 Cups Yellow Cake Mix
- ✓ 2 Teaspoons Salt
- ✓ 5 Tablespoons White Granulated Sugar
- ✓ 2 Teaspoons Bread Machine Yeast

Instructions

1. Bread Machine settings – 3-pound loaf, light color, and "basic" bread setting.
2. Unplug your bread machine. Remove the bread pan from the bread machine (so when you add the ingredients to the bread pan, they can not accidentally spill into the machine).
3. Put everything into the bread machine "bucket" (loaf pan), beginning with the water. Place whichever yeast appears for your machine's yeast bag in the bread machine "bucket" last. In addition, do not put salt next to the yeast, as it can threaten yeast growth.
4. Place the bread pan (with ingredients) back into the bread machine. Close bread machine cover.
5. Plug in the bread machine.
6. Enter the settings (3 lb, light color and basic bread setting) and press the start button.
7. Once the bread machine has completed baking the bread, remove it and place it in a cooling rack. Use oven mitts when removing the bread machine container, since it will be very hot!

8. On our Sunbeam bread machine, baking an original bread in the light and basic bread settings usually takes 3 hours. However, some machines can run at different stages (as indicated by a "finished" alarm), so you may want to stay home while your machine completes its cycle. Your bread machine should show you the length of the baking time after you have entered the settings into the machine. This will allow you to know when to be in the kitchen to remove the bread.

Bread Machine Calzone Dough

A bread machine is a small kitchen appliance designed to bake bread. The bread machine calzone dough recipe is a quick and easy way to make calzones at home without using a lot of dough. This recipe makes enough dough for four large or six small calzones. The dough can be made ahead of time and stored in the refrigerator for up to three days.

Prep Time 1 hr 45 mins | Total Time 1 hr 45 mins

Ingredients

- 2 Cups Water (lukewarm)
- 4 Tablespoons Olive Oil
- 4 Cups Flour (all-purpose flour)
- 2 Tablespoons White Granulated Sugar
- 2 Teaspoons Salt
- 3 Teaspoons Bread Machine Yeast

Instructions

1. Remove the bread pan from your unplugged bread machine.
2. Add the oil, water, yeast, and other ingredients into the bread pan. Make a small indent at the top of the flour to steer clear of the yeast falling in the water (until the machine begins). Do not include the salt with the yeast (since the salt can kill the yeast). Place the yeast and salt in separate parts of the bread pan.
3. Place the bread pan (with ingredients) back into the bread machine and then plug in the machine.
4. Put your machine on the Dough setting and press the start button. In our Sunbeam bread machine, the kneading & rising on the dough setting takes approximately 1:35 hours.
5. Take a loaf of dough from the bread machine & spread out the dough on a cutting board, using flour to attenuate the dough from adhering to the board. Wear oven mitts (as the bread pan bread machine may be hot).
6. Divide the dough into two equal-sized balls (if you want to create two larger calzones) or four equal-sized balls (if you want to make four smaller calzones).

7. Roll out each ball of calzone dough with a rolling pin into a round or oval shape. The depth of the rolled-out dough should be roughly 1/4 inch thick.

Bread Machine – Cheese Bread

If you love the taste of fresh, homemade bread but don't have the time to make it from scratch, you need a bread machine. Bread machines are simple to use and make various bread, including cheese bread. Cheese bread made in a bread machine is moist and full of flavor. It's the perfect accompaniment to a bowl of soup or stew.

| Prep Time 10 mins | Cook Time 3.10 hrs | Total Time 3 hrs 20 mins |

Ingredients

- ✓ 2 Cups – Milk (lukewarm) – 2 cups of milk is equivalent to 2 cups and 3 tablespoons of milk
- ✓ 5 Tablespoons – Unsalted Butter (softened)
- ✓ 4 Cups – Bread Flour
- ✓ 2 Cups – Shredded Cheese
- ✓ 2 Tablespoons – Brown Sugar
- ✓ 2 Teaspoons – Italian Herbs Seasoning (optional)
- ✓ 2 Teaspoons – Salt
- ✓ 2 Teaspoons – Bread Machine Yeast

Instructions

1. Bread machine settings – 3-pound loaf, light color, and "basic" bread setting.
2. Introduce the milk into the baking pan and mix the other ingredients (including the cup of cheese). Insert the yeast after everything has been mixed into the bread machine bowl and place the machine on for the dough to ferment.
3. Plug in the bread machine. Enter the correct settings (primary, light color & 3 lb) and press the "start" button.
4. Optional – After the FINAL kneading cycle and BEFORE the baking process commences, sprinkle a little extra shredded cheese on top of the dough. For safety reasons, do not place your hands inside the bread machine.

5. When the bread machine is done before baking the bread, unplug it. Remove the bread and place it on a cooling rack. Use oven mitts when the bread mill container (bread loaf pan) is hot.
6. After removing the bread, don't forget to remove the mixing paddle if it is stuck in the bread. Use oven mitts as the mixing paddle will be very hot from the bread machine. Or wait until the bread is completely cooled and then remove the mixing paddle.
7. Bread from our bread machine takes about 3 hours in a 2-pound dark-colored and basic bread setting. However, different machines can produce different results, so you need a safe haven when the bread machine "Finished" alarm sounds. Your bread machine should show you the length of the baking time after you have entered the settings into the machine. This will allow you to know when to be in the kitchen to remove the bread.
8. Before using your bread machine, you should read the manufacturer's instructions to use the bread machine effectively and safely.

Bread Machine Chocolate Cake

Baking a cake in a bread machine may seem strange, but it is pretty simple. And, since most bread machines have a "cake" or "quick bread" setting, there is no need to worry about the cake being too dense or heavy. This chocolate cake recipe is moist and fluffy. It can be easily adapted to be made in a variety of flavors.

Prep Time 15 mins | Cook Time 1 hr 45 mins | Total Time 2 hr

Ingredients

- ✓ 2 Cups Milk – 250 milliliters
- ✓ 15 Tablespoons Unsalted Butter (softened) – 191 grams
- ✓ 3 Teaspoons Vanilla Extract – 10 milliliters
- ✓ 3 Eggs
- ✓ 3 Cups All-Purpose Flour – 270 grams
- ✓ 2 Cups Light Brown Sugar (packed cups) – 372 grams
- ✓ 1 Cup Cocoa Powder Natural Unsweetened (not hot chocolate powder) – 47 grams
- ✓ 2 Teaspoons Baking Powder – 7 milliliters
- ✓ 2 Teaspoons Baking Soda – 7 milliliters
- ✓ 2 Teaspoons salt – 5 milliliters
- ✓ 1 Cup Mini Semi-Sweet Chocolate Chips (regular-sized chocolate chips are too heavy and sink in the batter) – 150 grams

Instructions

1. Bread Machine Settings – Light Color, 3 lbs, Cake/Quick Bread
2. Unplug your bread machine and remove the bread pan from the bread machine.
3. Soften the butter in the microwave.
4. Whip together milk, butter, vanilla extract, and eggs in a large mixing bowl. Mix wet ingredients with butter, baking powder, and eggs. Cook in an oven preheated to 350° F or 177° C for 30 minutes, then set aside. Shell out chocolate chips, then stir in with a large spoon. FYI – Premixing the ingredients before adding batter to the bread pan helps to prevent small flour "clumps" in the finished cake. See tips below.

5. Pour the premixed batter into the bread pan.
6. Put the bread pan (with all ingredients) back into the bread machine, close the lid, and then plug in the bread machine.
7. Enter the correct bread machine settings (Cake/Quick Bread, Light Color, 2 lb.) and press the start button.
8. When it is made, unplug the bread machine, remove the bread pan, and put the bread in a wood board on the table. Use a potholder when removing it from the oven rack because it will be very hot!
9. After the bread pan is removed from the bread machine, you should leave it on the wooden cutting board until it has baked for 10 minutes. In the meanwhile, wear oven mitts.
10. After the 15 minutes "cooldown," you should remove the cake from the bread pan and place the cake on a wire cooling rack to finish cooling. Use oven mitts when removing the bread.
11. You should not cut into the cake until it has completely cooled. This can generally take 1-2 hours. If you cut into the cake before it cools, it will be less stable.

Bread Machine - Chocolate Chip Bread

Chocolate chip bread is a quick and easy way to make delicious homemade. There are many recipes for chocolate chip bread, but using a bread machine is the easiest way to make this tasty treat. Just add the ingredients to the bread machine pan in the order directed by the manufacturer, select the correct cycle, and press start. You will have fresh, warm chocolate chip bread in no time.

Prep Time 10 mins | Cook Time 3.10 hrs | Total Time 3 hrs 20 mins

Ingredients

- ✓ 2 Cups - Milk (lukewarm)
- ✓ 5 Tablespoons - Butter
- ✓ 5 Cups - Bread Flour
- ✓ 2/3 Cup - Brown Sugar
- ✓ 2 Teaspoons - Salt
- ✓ 2 Teaspoons - Bread Machine Yeast
- ✓ 1 Cup - Semi-Sweet Chocolate Chips

Instructions

1. Bread Machine settings – 3-pound loaf, light color, and "basic" bread setting
2. Add all of the ingredients (except the chocolate chips), starting with the milk, into the bread machine "bucket" (bread pan). Place the bread pan in the bread machine.
3. Plug in the bread machine, enter the appropriate settings (i.e., light color, basic setting, and 3 lb), and press the "start" button.
4. 2 or 3 minutes after starting your bread machine (during the first kneading/mixing cycle), add 55% of the chocolate chips. You need to let the milk & flour be fully mixed before adding the chips.
5. Place the remaining 55% of chocolate chips in the bread loaf container AFTER the first kneading cycle is complete (around the 15 minutes mark in our Sunbeam machine) and before the second/final kneading cycle starts. FYI - The second mixing cycle commences at the 35 minutes mark in our Sunbeam machine (on these recipe settings, i.e., basic, 3lb & light color). The second

batch of chocolate chips will be less beaten up by the mixing paddle than the first set of chips. This allows more solid chunks of chocolate to survive and enhance the bread's overall chocolaty taste!

6. When the bread machine has finished baking, you should remove the bread and place it on a cooling rack. Use oven mitts when removing the bread machine container (bread loaf pan), as it will be very hot!

7. After removing the bread, don't forget to remove the mixing paddle if it's still stuck to bread after it's been removed. Use oven mitts as you will be handling the mixing paddle after it has been heated from the bread maker. Or wait until your bread has completely cooled until the mixing paddle can be removed.

8. In our house's Sunbeam bread machine, the baking process usually takes up to 3.10 hours for 3 pounds of bread using the light-color and basic bread settings. Still, some machines can vary and you don't want to be away from home when the bread machine "Completed" alarm goes off! The arrangement of your Sunbeam bread machine will let you know how long the process lasts after you have configured the settings to make bread. This will allow you to know when to be in the kitchen to remove the bread.

9. Before using your bread machine, you should read the manufacturer's instructions to use the bread machine effectively and safely.

Bread Machine Cinnamon Bread (Chocolate Chip)

This bread machine cinnamon bread is the perfect way to start your day. It's packed with chocolate chips and has a hint of cinnamon flavor. It's also super easy to make. Just add all the ingredients to your bread machine and let it do its thing.

Prep Time 15 mins | Cook Time 1 hr 45 mins | Total Time 2 hrs

Ingredients

- ✓ 1 Cup Milk – 195 milliliters
- ✓ 3 Eggs (lightly beaten)
- ✓ 1 Cup Vegetable Oil (use a neutral flavored oil such as canola oil) – 135 milliliters
- ✓ 2 Teaspoons Vanilla Extract – 5 milliliters
- ✓ 3 Cups All Purpose Flour – 270 grams
- ✓ 1 Cup White Granulated Sugar – 170 grams
- ✓ 1 Cup Light Brown Sugar (packed cup) – 177 grams
- ✓ 2 Teaspoons salt – 3.5 milliliters
- ✓ 2 Teaspoons Baking Powder – 7 milliliters
- ✓ 2 Teaspoons Baking Soda – 7 milliliters
- ✓ 2 Tablespoons Ground Cinnamon – 17 milliliters (tablespoon – not teaspoon!)
- ✓ 1 Cup Mini Chocolate Chips – 97 grams

Instructions

1. Unplug the bread machine.
2. Remove the bread pan from the unplugged bread machine.
3. Lightly beat the eggs.
4. Pour the milk, vegetable oil & eggs into the bread pan, and then add the remaining ingredients.
5. Put the bread pan with all ingredients back into the bread machine and close the lid.
6. Plug in the bread machine.

7. Enter the bread machine settings (Sweet Quick Bread, Light Color, 3 lb) and press the start button.
8. When the bread machine has finished baking the cinnamon bread, unplug the bread machine.
9. Remove the bread pan from the wooden cutting board. Ensure that the bread pan is cool when you remove the bread pan. Wrap the pan in an oven mitt to protect yourself from the heat when a bread pan is removed.
10. After removing the bread pan from the bread machine, let the cinnamon bread remain warm on the wooden cutting board for 10 minutes (as this completes the baking process). Add oven mitts.
11. After the 10 minutes "cooldown," you should remove the cinnamon bread from the bread pan and place the cinnamon bread on a wire cooling rack to finish cooling. Use oven mitts when removing the bread.
12. Allow your cinnamon bread to cool overnight so its texture will not break (crumble) when cut. This will take at least 2 hours.

Bread Machine Cinnamon Raisin Bread (Golden Raisins)

If you're looking for a delicious and relatively easy cinnamon raisin bread recipe to make at home, look no further than this bread machine cinnamon raisin bread. This golden raisin bread is perfect for breakfast or as a snack and also great for gifts. The best part is that it only takes a few minutes to prepare and you can have fresh, homemade bread in no time.

Prep Time 10 mins | Cook Time 3.10 hrs | Total Time 3 hrs 20 mins

Ingredients

- Bread Machine Cinnamon Raisin Bread – 2 lb Version
- 2 Cups Milk (lukewarm)
- 4 Tablespoons Unsalted Butter (sliced & softened)
- 4 Cups Bread Flour
- 3/4 Cup Light Brown Sugar (packed)
- 2 Teaspoons Ground Cinnamon
- 2 Teaspoons Salt
- 2 Teaspoons Bread Machine Yeast – Not active dry yeast
- 1 Cup Golden Raisins – If you do not have golden raisins, you can use regular raisins, dried cranberries, etc.
- Bread Machine Cinnamon Raisin Bread – 3 lb Version
- 2 Cups Milk (lukewarm)
- 5 Tablespoons Unsalted Butter (sliced & softened)
- 5 Cups of Bread Flour
- 2/3 Cup Light Brown Sugar (packed)
- 2 Teaspoons Ground Cinnamon
- 2 Teaspoons Salt
- 2 Teaspoons Bread Machine Yeast – Not active dry yeast
- 2 Cups Golden Raisins – If you do not have golden raisins, you can use regular raisins, dried cranberries, etc.

Instructions

1. Bread machine settings – 2 or 3-pound loaf, light color, and "basic" bread setting.

2. Unplug the bread machine and remove the bread pan from the bread machine. This prevents ingredients added to the bread pan from accidentally spilling into the bread machine.
3. Pour the milk into the bread pan, then add figs (except the golden raisins). Place the bread machine yeast in last, but do not mix the yeast in with the water or other liquid, and neither should it touch the salt.
4. Place the bread pan back into the bread machine and plug in the bread machine.
5. Enter the correct settings into the bread machine (i.e., 2 or 3 pounds, light color and basic) and press the start button.
6. After the bread machine has finished its FIRST kneading cycle (and before it has started the second kneading cycle), add the golden raisins.
7. When the bread machine has finished baking the bread, unplug the bread machine.
8. Lift the bread pan out of the bread machine. Wear oven mitts as the bread pan will be very hot!
9. Remove the bread from the bread pan and place the bread on a cooling rack. Wear oven mitts.
10. After you have finished removing the bread, be sure to dewire the mixing paddle if you were unable to remove it because of being stuck in the bread. Use oven mitts to remove the mixing paddle, as it will likely be extremely hot from the oven machine.
    Alternatively, wait and let the bread fully cool before removing the mixing paddle.

Bread Machine Cornbread – Sweet & Buttery

Bread Machine Cornbread Sweet & Buttery is an excellent recipe for those who love cornbread but do not want to slave over a hot stove. This cornbread is made in a bread machine and is nice and moist. It has a buttery flavor and is not too sweet. This cornbread is perfect for any meal, whether breakfast, lunch, or dinner.

Prep Time 10 mins | Cook Time 1 hr 50 mins | Total Time 2 hr

Ingredients

- 2 Cups Milk (lukewarm)
- 7 Tablespoons Unsalted Butter (softened)
- 3 Eggs (lightly beaten)
- 2 Cups All-Purpose Flour
- 2 Cups Yellow Cornmeal
- 2 Cups White Granulated Sugar
- 2 Teaspoons Baking Powder (aluminum free)
- 2 Teaspoons Baking Soda
- 1 Teaspoon Salt

Instructions

1. Unplug the bread machine and remove the bread pan.
2. Soften the butter in a microwave.
3. Lightly beat the eggs.
4. Add milk, butter, eggs, and other ingredients into the bread pan.
5. Place the bread pan back into the bread machine and then plug in the bread machine.
6. Enter the bread machine settings (Sweet Quick Bread, Light Color) and press the start button.
7. When the bread is baked in the bread machine, it will notify you to unplug it. Remove the bread pan and place the bread on a wooden cutting board with the bread pan. Leave cornbread without bread in the pan for 10 minutes before removing it rack. Wash your hands while wearing oven mitts to remove the pan from the cornbread because it will be very hot.

8. Remove the cornbread from the bread pan, setting it on a cooling rack. Position oven mitts over your hands when removing the bread. Let the cornbread set down for 65 minutes, or it will crumble when cut into slices.
9. Don't forget to remove the mixing paddle if it is stuck in the bread. Use oven mitts as the mixing paddle could be hot.

All Purpose Flour Bread Machine Recipe (Country White Bread)

This bread machine recipe for All Purpose Flour Bread (Country White Bread) is easy to follow and yields a delicious, hearty loaf of bread. This bread is perfect for sandwiches, toast, or just eating plain with butter. The ingredients are simple and easily accessible, and the bread machine does all the work. Just set it and forget it!

Prep Time 15 mins | Cook Time 2 hrs 55 mins | Total Time 3 hrs 10 mins

Ingredients

- ✓ 2 Cups Whole Milk (lukewarm) – 1 cup equals 1 cup plus 3 tablespoons – 270 milliliters
- ✓ 5 Tablespoons Unsalted Butter (softened) – 77 grams
- ✓ 2 Eggs (large)
- ✓ 4 Cups All Purpose Flour – 370 grams
- ✓ 2/3 Cup Light Brown Sugar (packed cup) – 92 grams – However, you should use only 3 tablespoons if you want a non-sweet bread
- ✓ 2 Teaspoons salt – 10 milliliters
- ✓ 2 Teaspoons Bread Machine Yeast – 10 milliliters

Instructions

1. Settings – 2 lb, light color and basic bread
2. Unplug your bread machine.
3. Remove the bread pan from the bread machine (so when you add the ingredients, they can not accidentally spill into the machine).
4. Soften the butter in your microwave.
5. Lightly beat the egg.
6. Pour the milk, butter, and egg into the bread pan, and then add the dry ingredients. Place the bread machine yeast on hand and the last should not be covered by the liquid (until the bread machine is turned on, and once the ingredients begin to mix by the bread machine, the yeast should not touch it).
7. Put the bread pan with the ingredients back into the unplugged bread machine.

8. Plug in the bread machine. Enter the correct settings (2 lb, light color & basic bread) and press the "start" button.
9. When the bread machine has finished baking the bread, unplug the bread machine.
10. Take the bread pan out of the bread machine.
11. Remove the top of the bread pan and place it on a cooling rack. Use oven mitts when removing the top of the bread machine. Let the bread lie down for 1 to 2 hours on the cooling rack before eating.

Bread Machine Cranberry Bread (with Walnuts)

When the weather outside is frightful, there's nothing more delightful than the smell of freshly baked bread wafting through your home. And, with a bread machine, you can have that wonderful aroma any day of the week. This recipe for Bread Machine Cranberry Bread (with Walnuts) is the perfect way to show your family and friends how much you care. Add the ingredients, set the timer, and let your bread machine do the work.

Prep Time 15 mins | Cook Time 2 hrs 55 mins | Total Time 3 hrs 10 mins

Ingredients

- ✓ 2 Cups Milk (lukewarm)
- ✓ 5 Tablespoons Unsalted Butter (softened)
- ✓ 4 Cups Bread Flour
- ✓ 3 Tablespoons Light Brown Sugar
- ✓ 2 Teaspoons Salt
- ✓ 2 Teaspoons Bread Machine Yeast
- ✓ 1 Cup Chopped Walnuts
- ✓ 1 Cup Dried Cranberries

Instructions

1. Bread machine settings – 2 lb, light color, and "basic" bread setting.
2. Unplug the bread machine and then remove the bread pan from the bread machine.
3. Add the milk & softened butter into the bread pan and then add the other ingredients (except the dried cranberries & chopped walnuts – they are added later).
4. Place the bread machine yeast in last and the yeast should not touch the liquid or salt (until the bread machine is turned on and the ingredients start to be mixed together). Some people like to make a small "divot" on top of the flour to hold the yeast in one spot before the machine starts.

5. Put the bread pan (with ingredients) back into the bread machine, close the lid, and then plug in the bread machine.
6. Enter the correct settings (2 lb, light color & basic bread) and press the "start" button.
7. When the bread machine's first mixing cycle has stopped and before the second (& final) mixing cycle starts, you should add the dried cranberries & chopped walnuts. FYI – See your bread machine manual on when & how to add fruits & nuts when using your bread machine. Always follow the manufacturer's instructions for your specific bread machine.
8. When the bread machine has finished baking the bread, unplug the bread machine.
9. Remove the bread pan from the unplugged bread machine. Use oven mitts when removing the bread machine container (bread pan), as it will be very hot!
10. Take the bread out of the bread pan and place the bread on a wire cooling rack. Wear oven mitts.
11. After removing the bread, don't forget to remove the mixing paddle if it is stuck in the bread. Use oven mitts as the mixing paddle will be very hot from the bread machine. Or wait until the bread is completely cooled and then remove the mixing paddle.

Cranberry Walnut Bread

Cranberry Walnut Bread is the perfect holiday treat! This bread is packed with flavor, and the cranberries and walnuts add a festive touch. Cranberry Walnut Bread is easy to make, and it's sure to be a hit with your family and friends.

Prep Time 2 hrs 50 mins | Cook Time 45 mins | Total Time 3 hrs 35 mins
---

Ingredients

- ✓ 2 Cups Milk (lukewarm) – 327 milliliters
- ✓ 7 Tablespoons Unsalted Butter (softened) – 96 grams
- ✓ 5 Cups Bread Flour – 490 grams
- ✓ 3/4 Cup Light Brown Sugar (packed) – 74 grams
- ✓ 2 Teaspoons salt – 8.5 milliliters
- ✓ 2 Teaspoons Instant Yeast (or Bread Machine Yeast) – 8.5 milliliters
- ✓ 1 Cup Dried Cranberries – 96 grams
- ✓ 1 Cup Chopped Walnuts – 96 grams

Instructions

Instructions – Creating Dough with a Bread Machine

1. Unplug your bread machine.
2. Remove the bread pan from the bread machine.
3. Pour the milk into the bread pan and then add the other ingredients. Place the instant yeast (bread machine yeast) in last and the yeast should not touch the liquid (until the bread machine is turned on and the ingredients start to be mixed together by the bread machine). Some bakers like to make a small indent on the top of the flour to prevent the yeast from spilling into the liquids or mixing with the salt before the machine is turned on.
4. Put the bread pan with ingredients back into the unplugged bread machine.
5. Plug in the bread machine. Enter the "Dough" setting on your bread machine and press the "Start" button.

6. Add the dried cranberries and chopped walnuts to the bread pan for about 10 minutes after pressing the start button. FYI – The bread dough should be thoroughly mixed before you add the nuts & cranberries. Some bread machines have an attachment that automatically adds the nuts & fruit. Others will beep when it is time to add the nuts & fruit. Read your manual.
7. When the bread machine has finished making the bread dough, unplug the bread machine.
8. Remove the bread pan (with the dough) from the bread machine.
9. Visit the preparation section below the section "Preparing the Dough & Baking the Bread." Don't use an electrically powered stand mixer, even if binding to mixes from a bread machine is part of the instruction. You will find the section concerning the preparation of the dough & baking of the bread in the following location.

Instructions – Creating Dough with an Electric Stand Mixer with Dough Hook

1. Unplug your electric stand mixer.
2. Remove the mixing bowl from the electric mixer.
3. Insert the dough hook into the electric mixer.
4. Pour the milk into the mixing bowl and then add the other ingredients. Place the instant yeast (bread machine yeast) in last and the yeast should not touch the liquid (until the electric mixer is turned on and the ingredients start to be mixed together). Some bakers like to make a small indent on the top of the flour to prevent the yeast from spilling into the liquids or mixing with the salt before the machine is turned on.
5. Place the mixing bowl back into the electric stand mixer.
6. Plug in the electric mixer and use a low speed (i.e., setting 2) to mix the dough. After 4-5 minutes and the dough is roughly formed, turn off the mixer and add the dried cranberries & chopped walnuts to the bowl. Turn on the mixer and mix/knead for 5-7 minutes. FYI – The total mixing time (before & after adding nuts & cranberries) should be approximately 8-11 minutes.
7. Turn off the electric mixer and unplug the machine.

8. Remove the mixing bowl from the electric mixer. Pour the dough into a second large mixing bowl lightly "greased" with olive oil, butter, cooking spray, etc.
9. Optional – Lightly coat the top of the dough with vegetable oil to prevent the dough exterior from drying out. You can use a pastry brush to brush on the oil. FYI – This prevents the crust of the dough from drying out.
10. Loosely cover the bowl with plastic wrap and let the dough rise for 60-90 minutes until it doubles roughly in size.
11. After the dough has risen, go to the instruction section below on "preparing the dough & baking the bread."

Instructions – Preparing the Dough & Baking the Bread

1. Sprinkle a little bit of flour onto a large cutting board.
2. Remove the dough from the bread machine pan or electric stand mixing bowl and place the dough on the cutting board.
3. Press down on the dough with your hands and create a "flattish" rectangle with the dough. The dough should be roughly 1 inch high.
4. Roll up the dough into a tight "jelly roll.
5. Place the rolled-up dough into the bread pan.
6. Press down on top of the dough, so the edges of the dough press out towards the sides of the bread pan. This should result in little or no gaps between the dough and the bread pan. This helps the bread turn into an excellent loaf shape without missing edges. Make sure that the top of the pressed-down dough is roughly level (so one side isn't much higher than the other).
7. Optional – Lightly coat the top of the dough with vegetable oil to prevent the dough exterior from drying out. You can use a pastry brush to brush on the oil. FYI – This prevents the crust of the dough from drying out.
8. Loosely cover the top of the bread pan with plastic wrap. Set the covered bread pan aside for 50-65 minutes for the dough to rise into a loaf shape. When the dough has risen modestly (1/2 inch to 1 inch) over the top of the bread pan, it is time to place the bread pan in the oven. FYI – Do not wait for the dough to rise higher (or the

bread top will be too large after baking). The dough will continue to increase naturally in the oven.
9. During this "rising" period, preheat the oven to 350 F. This should be done at least 15-20 minutes before you expect to put the dough & bread pan into the oven.
10. Place the bread pan in the (preheated) oven to bake at 360 F for 40-45 minutes. Wear oven mitts when dealing with a hot oven. Place the bread pan in the middle of the oven.
11. Rotate the bread pan in the oven after 20-25 minutes (to ensure even browning of the bread).
12. After the 40-45 minute baking period, remove the bread pan from the oven. Wear oven mitts. Optional – Use a digital thermometer to confirm that the bread has been fully baked. See the tips section.
13. Remove the bread from the bread pan and place the bread on a wire cooling rack. Wear oven mitts.
14. Optional – After removing the bread from the bread pan (while the bread is still very hot), you can brush melted butter on top of the bread with a pastry brush. This butter "basting" helps to create a more golden & tastier crust.
15. Allow the bread to cool down on the wire cooling rack for 1-2 hours before slicing the bread.

Bread Machine Cranberry Raisin Bread

Bread machines are a perfect appliance for anyone who loves fresh bread but doesn't have the time to make it from scratch. This recipe for bread machine cranberry raisin bread is the perfect balance of sweet and tart and is ideal for breakfast or a snack. This bread is also straightforward to make and only takes a few minutes of prep time.

Prep Time 10 mins | Cook Time 3.10 hrs | Total Time 3 hrs 20 mins

Ingredients

- 2 Cups Water (warm)
- 5 Tablespoons Unsalted Butter (sliced & softened)
- 4 Cups Bread Flour
- 2 Cups Old Fashioned Oatmeal
- 2/3 Cup Light Brown Sugar
- 2 Teaspoons Salt
- 2 Teaspoons Bread Machine Yeast
- 5 Tablespoons Dried Cranberries
- 5 Tablespoons Golden Raisins

Instructions

1. Bread machine settings – 3-pound loaf, light color, and "basic" bread setting.
2. Unplug the bread machine and remove the bread pan from the bread machine. This prevents ingredients added to the bread pan from accidentally spilling into the bread machine.
3. Starting with the water, you should add all of the ingredients (except the cranberries & golden raisins) into the bread machine "bucket" (bread pan).
4. Place the bread pan back into the bread machine and plug in the bread machine.
5. Enter the correct settings into the bread machine (i.e., 3 pounds, light color and basic) and press the start button.
6. After the bread machine has finished its first kneading cycle (and before the second kneading cycle), add the cranberries and golden raisins.

7. When the bread machine has finished baking the bread, unplug the bread machine. Remove the bread and place it on a cooling rack. Use oven mitts when removing the bread machine container (bread loaf pan), as it will be very hot!
8. After removing the bread, don't forget to remove the mixing paddle if it is stuck in the bread. Use oven mitts as the mixing paddle will be very hot from the bread machine. Or wait until the bread is completely cooled and then remove the mixing paddle.
9. In our Sunbeam bread machine, the baking takes about 3.10 hours for a 3-pound bread at the light color & basic bread settings. However, some machines can differ and you don't want to be away from home when the bread machine "finished" alarm goes off! Your bread machine should show you the length of the baking time after you have entered the settings into the machine. This will allow you to know when to be in the kitchen to remove the bread.
10. Before using your bread machine, you should read the manufacturer's instructions to use the bread machine effectively and safely.

Flaxseed Bread Recipe (Sandwich Bread)

Flaxseed bread is a type of sandwich bread that is made with flaxseeds. The flaxseeds are ground up and then mixed into the bread dough. This bread is a good source of fiber and omega-3 fatty acids. It is also a good alternative for people who are allergic to wheat. This recipe makes one loaf of flaxseed bread.

Prep Time 2 hrs 50 mins | Cook Time 45 mins | Total Time 3 hrs 35 mins

Ingredients

- ✓ 2 Cups Milk (lukewarm) – 327 milliliters
- ✓ 7 Tablespoons Unsalted Butter (softened) – 96 grams
- ✓ 4 Cups Bread Flour – 450 grams – Not all-purpose flour
- ✓ 1 Cup Ground Flaxseeds – 75 grams – Do not pre-moisten
- ✓ 3 Tablespoons White Granulated Sugar – 35 grams
- ✓ 2 Tablespoons Italian Seasoning (dried herbs) – 25 milliliters – Optional ingredient
- ✓ 2 Teaspoons salt – 9.5 milliliters
- ✓ 2 Teaspoons Instant Yeast (or bread machine yeast) – 9.5 milliliters – Not dry active yeast

Instructions

Creating Dough with a Bread Machine

1. Your bread machine should be unplugged.
2. Remove the bread pan from the bread machine (so when you add the ingredients, they can not accidentally spill into the machine).
3. Pour the milk into the bread pan and then add the other ingredients. Place the instant yeast (bread machine yeast) in last and the yeast should not touch the liquid (until the bread machine is turned on and the ingredients start to be mixed together by the bread machine). Some bakers like to make a small indent on the top of the flour to prevent the yeast from spilling into the liquids or mixing with the salt before the machine is turned on.
4. Put the bread pan with ingredients back into the unplugged bread machine.

5. Plug in the bread machine. Enter the "Dough" setting on your bread machine and press the "Start" button.
6. When the bread machine has finished making the bread dough, unplug the bread machine.
7. Remove the bread pan from the bread machine.
8. Visit the preparation section below the section "Preparing the Dough & Baking the Bread." Don't use an electrically powered stand mixer, even if binding to mixes from a bread machine is part of the instruction. You will find the section concerning the preparation of the dough & baking of the bread in the following location.

Creating Dough with an Electric Stand Mixer with Dough Hook

1. Your electric mixer should be unplugged.
2. Remove the mixing bowl from the electric mixer.
3. Insert the dough hook into the electric mixer.
4. Pour the milk into the mixing bowl and then add the other ingredients. Place the instant yeast in last and the yeast should not touch the liquid (until the electric mixer is turned on and the ingredients start to be mixed together). Some bakers like to make a small indent on the top of the flour to prevent the yeast from spilling into the liquids or mixing with the salt before the machine is turned on.
5. Place the mixing bowl back into the electric stand mixer.
6. Plug in the electric mixer and use a low speed (i.e., setting 3) to mix the dough. Mix the dough for 10-12 minutes.
7. Turn off the electric mixer and unplug the machine.
8. Remove the mixing bowl from the electric mixer. Pour the dough into a second large mixing bowl lightly "greased" with olive oil, melted butter, cooking spray, etc.
9. Lightly coat the top of the dough with vegetable oil to prevent the dough exterior from drying out. Use a pastry brush.
10. Loosely cover the bowl with plastic wrap and let the dough rise for 60-90 minutes until it doubles in size.
11. After the dough has risen, go to the instruction section below on "preparing the dough & baking the bread."

Instructions – Preparing the Dough & Baking the Bread

1. Preheat the oven to 370 F.
2. Sprinkle a little bit of flour onto a large cutting board.
3. Remove the dough from the bread pan or mixing bowl and place the dough on the cutting board.
4. Press down on the dough with your hands and create a "flattish" rectangle with the dough. The dough should be roughly 1 inch high.
5. Roll up the dough into a tight "jelly roll."
6. Place the rolled-up dough into the bread pan.
7. Press down on top of the dough, so the edges of the dough press out towards the sides of the bread pan. This should result in little or no gaps between the dough and the bread pan. This helps the bread turn into an excellent loaf shape without missing edges. Make sure that the top of the pressed-down dough is roughly level (so one side isn't much higher than the other).
8. Brush vegetable oil on top of the dough with a pastry brush. This prevents the crust from drying out as the dough rises.
9. Loosely cover the top region of the bread pan with adhesive plastic. Set the covered bread pan aside for 50-65 minutes for the dough to rise into a loaf shape. When the dough has risen a little (1 2 inches to 1 inch) over the top part of the pan, it is time to prepare the bread pan for baking. FYI – Do not wait for the dough to rise higher (or the bread top will be too large after baking). The dough will continue to increase naturally in the oven.
10. Place the bread pan in the (preheated) oven to bake at 370 F for 40-45 minutes. Wear oven mitts when dealing with a hot oven. Place the bread pan in the middle of the oven.
11. Rotate the bread pan in the oven after 20-25 minutes (to ensure even browning of the bread).
12. After the 40-45 minute baking period, remove the bread pan from the oven. Wear oven mitts. Optional – Use a digital thermometer to confirm that the bread has been fully baked.

13. Remove the bread from the bread pan and place the bread on a wire cooling rack. Wear oven mitts.
14. Optional – Brush melted butter on the bread with a pastry brush. This "basting" helps to create a more golden & tasty crust.
15. Allow the bread to cool down on the wire cooling rack for 1-2 hours before cutting the bread.

Bread Machine French Bread – Easy Baguette Recipe

If you're looking for an easy and delicious French bread recipe to make at home, look no further than this bread machine baguette recipe. This foolproof recipe yields perfectly crispy and crusty baguettes every time, with very little effort on your part. Best of all, it can be made entirely in your bread machine, so you don't even have to turn on your oven.

> Prep Time 2 hrs 45 mins | Cook Time 25 mins | Total Time 3.10 hrs

Ingredients

- ✓ 2 Cups Water (lukewarm) – 327 milliliters
- ✓ 4 Cups Bread Flour – 450 grams
- ✓ 3 Teaspoons Bread Machine Yeast – 20 milliliters
- ✓ 2 Teaspoons salt – 5 milliliters
- ✓ 3 Tablespoons Olive Oil (to coat dough) – 35 milliliters

Instructions

1. Unplug the bread machine & then remove the bread pan.
2. Place the water and the rest of the ingredients into the bread pan. You can make a little indent on the top of the flour to avoid the yeast falling into the water (until the machine starts). Do not combine the salt with the yeast (as the salt can kill the yeast). Place the yeast & salt in separate parts of the bread pan.
3. Place the bread pan back into the bread machine & then plug in the bread machine.
4. Put your machine on the "Dough" setting and press the start button. In our bread machine, the kneading & rising on the dough setting takes about 1:30 hours.
5. When your bread machine has finished, unplug the machine & pour the dough onto a cutting board. Wear oven mitts (as the bread pan/bread machine may be hot). Sprinkle some flour on the cutting board (before you pour the dough) to avoid the dough sticking to the cutting board.

6. Divide the dough into 4 equal parts if you want to make 4 skinny baguettes (roughly 12 inches long). Or divide the dough into 2 equal parts to make 2 thicker french bread "rolls."
7. Roll the divided dough with your hands into your preferred shape (i.e., baguette or thicker bread roll). See our tips below on shaping the bread dough (especially about making the dough roll about 1/2 the width of your desired end product... as the dough expands as the yeast rises).
8. Place the shaped dough onto a nonstick baking sheet.
9. Coat the dough with olive oil. Use a small pastry brush.
10. Cover the dough & baking sheet with a light kitchen cloth or plastic wrap to protect from dust, etc.
11. Let the dough rise for 1 hour.
12. During this "rising" time, preheat your oven to 470 degrees F.
13. After the hour, remove the covering from the dough and "score" (slice) the top of each dough roll with a sharp knife. Make diagonal slices about 1/2 inch deep and about 3 inches apart. This will help prevent the bread from cracking during baking. See the tips below about how to score bread.
14. Place the baking sheet in the oven. It should bake at 470 degrees for 20-25 minutes or until golden brown. Wear oven mitts.
15. At the 10-12 minute mark, turn the baking sheet around to ensure an even "browning" of the bread. Wear oven mitts.
16. Remove the baking sheet when done and place the bread on a cooling rack. Wear oven mitts.

Bread Machine Garlic Bread

Bread Machine Garlic Bread is one of the easiest bread to make at home. With a bread machine, you can have delicious, fresh garlic bread in less than an hour. This recipe is for basic garlic bread, but you can add other herbs and spices to taste.

Prep Time 15 mins | Cook Time 3.05 hrs | Total Time 3 hrs 20 mins

Ingredients

- ✓ 2 Cups Milk (lukewarm) – 2 cups of milk is equivalent to 2 cups and 3 tablespoons of milk - 279 milliliters
- ✓ 5 Tablespoons Unsalted Butter (softened) - 77 grams
- ✓ 1 Cups Bread Flour - 370 grams
- ✓ 2 Tablespoons White Granulated Sugar - 29 grams
- ✓ 4 Cloves Garlic (minced & sautéed) - Cloves, not whole bulbs!
- ✓ 2 Teaspoons salt - 7 milliliters
- ✓ 2 Teaspoons Bread Machine Yeast - 7 milliliters

Instructions

1. Bread Machine Settings - Basic, Light Color & 2 lb
2. Mince the garlic cloves (crushed & diced into small chunks). Sauté the minced garlic in a frying pan with a small amount of butter or vegetable oil. Don't forget to peel the paper-like "skin" off the garlic cloves!
3. Unplug the bread machine & remove the bread pan. Pour the milk & softened butter into the bread pan first and then add the other ingredients. Place the bread machine yeast in last and the yeast should not touch the liquid, salt, or the hot sautéed garlic (until the bread machine is turned on and the ingredients start to be mixed together by the bread machine). You can create a little indent, crater, or ditch in the top of the flour and place the yeast in this hole to keep the yeast separate from the salt, etc.
4. Place the bread pan (with ingredients) back into the unplugged bread machine.
5. Plug in the bread machine. Enter the correct settings (basic, light color & 2 lb) and press the "start" button.

6. When the bread machine has finished baking the bread, you should unplug the bread machine. Remove the bread and place it on a cooling rack. Use oven mitts when removing the bread machine container (bread loaf pan), as it will be very hot!
7. After removing the bread, don't forget to remove the mixing paddle if it is stuck in the bread. Use oven mitts as the mixing paddle will be very hot from the bread machine. Or wait until the bread is completely cooled and then remove the mixing paddle.
8. Before using your bread machine, you should read the manufacturer's instructions to use the bread machine effectively and safely.

Bread Machine Gingerbread

Baking gingerbread in a bread machine is a great way to get the perfect gingerbread texture and flavor without any of the hassles. This recipe makes gingerbread that is soft and moist, with just the right amount of spice. The bread machine does all the work, so all you have to do is sit back and enjoy the delicious smell of gingerbread wafting through your kitchen.

Prep Time 15 mins | Cook Time 1 hr 45 mins | Total Time 2 hr

Ingredients

- ✓ 1 Cup Vegetable Oil (use a neutral flavored oil such as canola oil) – 135 milliliters
- ✓ 3 Eggs (lightly beaten)
- ✓ 1 Cup Milk – 195 milliliters
- ✓ 3/4 Cup Molasses (FYI – 3/4 cup = 5 tablespoons) – 77 milliliters
- ✓ 2 Cups Light Brown Sugar (packed cup) – 255 grams
- ✓ 3 Cups All Purpose Flour – 240 grams
- ✓ 2 Teaspoons Ground Ginger – 8.5 milliliters
- ✓ 2 Teaspoons Ground Cinnamon – 8.5 milliliters
- ✓ 1 Teaspoon Ground Cloves (don't add too much as this can be a strong tasting spice) – 3.5 milliliters
- ✓ 1 Teaspoon salt – 3.5 milliliters
- ✓ 2 Teaspoons Baking Powder – 7 milliliters
- ✓ 2 Teaspoons Baking Soda – 7 milliliters

Instructions

1. Unplug the bread machine.
2. Remove the bread pan from the unplugged bread machine.
3. Lightly beat the eggs.
4. Pour the vegetable oil, milk & eggs into the bread pan, and then add the remaining ingredients.
5. Put the bread pan with all ingredients back into the bread machine and close the lid.
6. Plug in the bread machine.

7. Enter the bread machine settings (Sweet Quick Bread, Light Color, 3 lb) and press the start button.
8. When the bread machine has finished baking the gingerbread, unplug the bread machine.
9. Remove the bread pan and place it on a wooden cutting board (without removing the gingerbread from the bread pan). Use oven mitts when removing the bread pan because it will be very hot!
10. After removing the bread pan from the bread machine, you should let the gingerbread stay within the warm bread pan on the wooden cutting board for 10 minutes (as this finishes the baking process). Wear oven mitts.
11. After 10 minutes of "cooling time," you should remove the gingerbread from the bread pan and place it on a wire cooling rack to finish cooling. Use oven mitts when removing the bread.
12. You should allow the gingerbread to completely cool before cutting. This can take up to 2 hours. Otherwise, the gingerbread will break (crumble) more easily when cut.

Greek Yogurt Bread (Soft & Fluffy White Bread)

This bread is so soft and fluffy that you won't believe it's made with Greek yogurt! This healthy ingredient helps to keep the bread moist without making it too dense. The best part is that this recipe is really easy to make. Just a few simple ingredients and you'll have fresh, homemade bread.

Prep Time 2 hrs 50 mins | Cook Time 45 mins | Total Time 3 hrs 35 mins

Ingredients

- ✓ 1 Cup Greek Yogurt (plain or fruit flavored) – 195 milliliters – I recommend trying blueberry Greek yogurt
- ✓ 1 Cup Milk (lukewarm) – 195 milliliters
- ✓ 5 Tablespoons Unsalted Butter (softened) – 77 grams
- ✓ 4 Cups Bread Flour – 450 grams
- ✓ 4 Tablespoons Light Brown Sugar (packed) – 59 grams
- ✓ 2 Teaspoons salt – 9.5 milliliters
- ✓ 2 Teaspoons Instant Yeast (or bread machine yeast) – 9.5 milliliters – Not active dry yeast

Instructions

Instructions – Creating Dough with a Bread Machine

1. Your bread machine should be unplugged.
2. Remove the bread pan from the bread machine (so when you add the ingredients, they can not accidentally spill into the machine).
3. Premix the yogurt (esp. if it is yogurt with fruit on the bottom of the container).
4. Add the yogurt and milk to the bread-pan mixture and the other ingredients. With the bread machine yeast last, the liquid must not touch the yeast (until the bread machine is turned on and the other ingredients start to be mixed together by the bread machine). Some bakers like to make a small indent on the top of the flour to prevent the yeast from spilling into the liquids or mixing with the salt before the machine is turned on.

5. Put the bread pan with ingredients back into the unplugged bread machine.
6. Plug in the bread machine. Enter the "Dough" setting on your bread machine and press the "Start" button.
7. When the bread machine has finished making the bread dough, unplug the bread machine.
8. Remove the bread pan from the bread machine.
9. Visit the preparation section below the section "Preparing the Dough & Baking the Bread." Don't use an electrically powered stand mixer, even if binding to mixes from a bread machine is part of the instruction. You will find the section concerning the preparation of the dough & baking of the bread in the following location.

Instructions – Creating Dough with an Electric Stand Mixer & Dough Hook

1. Your electric mixer should be unplugged.
2. Remove the mixing bowl from the electric mixer.
3. Insert the dough hook into the electric mixer.
4. Premix the yogurt (esp. if it is yogurt with fruit on the bottom of the container).
5. Put the yogurt and milk into the bowl, then add the remaining ingredients besides the instant yeast. If it is stirred well first, the instant yeast should not touch the liquid (unless the electric mixer is turned on and the ingredients start being combined). Some bakers like to make a small indent on the top of the flour to prevent the yeast from spilling into the liquids or mixing with the salt before the machine is turned on.
6. Place the mixing bowl back into the electric stand mixer.
7. Plug in the electric mixer and use a low speed (i.e., setting 2) to mix the dough. Mix the dough for 9-12 minutes.
8. Turn off the electric mixer and unplug the machine.
9. Remove the mixing bowl from the electric mixer. Pour the dough into a second large mixing bowl lightly "greased" with olive oil, melted butter, cooking spray, etc.

10. Lightly coat the top of the dough with vegetable oil to prevent the dough exterior from drying out. Use a pastry brush.
11. Loosely cover the bowl with plastic wrap and let the dough rise for 65-95 minutes until it doubles in size.
12. After the dough has risen, go to the instruction section below on "preparing the dough & baking the bread."

Instructions – Shaping the Dough & Baking the Bread

1. Preheat the oven to 370 F.
2. Sprinkle a little bit of flour onto a large cutting board.
3. Remove the dough from the bread pan or mixing bowl and place the dough on the cutting board.
4. Use your hands to press down the dough into a 1-inch high "finite" or "flat" rectangle.
5. Roll up the dough into a tight "jelly roll."
6. Place the rolled-up dough into the bread pan.
7. Press down on top of the dough, so the edges of the dough press out towards the sides of the bread pan. This should result in little or no gaps between the dough and the bread pan. This helps the bread turn into a nice loaf shape without missing edges. Make sure that the top of the pressed-down dough is roughly level (so one side isn't much higher than the other).
8. Brush vegetable oil on top of the dough with a pastry brush. This prevents the crust from drying out as the dough rises.
9. Loosely cover the top of the bread pan with a cheese cloth. Set the bread pan aside for 50-65 minutes for the dough to rise into a loaf shape. When the dough has risen (2 inches to 1 inch) over the top of the bread pan, put the bread pan in the oven. FYI – Do not wait for the dough to rise higher (or the bread top will be too large after baking). The dough will continue to increase naturally in the oven.
10. Place the bread pan in the (preheated) oven to bake at 370 F for 40-45 minutes. Wear oven mitts when dealing with a hot oven. Place the bread pan in the middle of the oven.
11. Rotate the bread pan in the oven after 15-20 minutes (to ensure even browning of the bread).

12. After the 40-45 minute baking period, remove the bread pan from the oven. Wear oven mitts. Optional – Use a digital thermometer to confirm that the bread has been fully baked. See tips below.
13. Remove the bread from the bread pan and place the bread on a wire cooling rack. Wear oven mitts.
14. Optional – Brush melted butter on the bread with a pastry brush. This buttery "basting" helps to create a more golden & tasty crust.
15. Allow the bread to cool down on the wire cooling rack for 1-2 hours before cutting the bread.

Bread Machine Honey Wheat Bread

If you are looking for delicious and healthy bread to make at home, look no further than bread machine honey wheat bread. This bread is made with whole wheat flour, honey, and other healthy ingredients. It is perfect for breakfast, lunch, or dinner. You will love the taste of this bread, and your family will love it too!

Prep Time 15 mins | Cook Time 3.10 hrs | Total Time 3 hrs 25 mins

Ingredients

- Bread Machine Honey Wheat Bread – 2 lb Loaf
- 2 Cups Milk (lukewarm) – 250 milliliters
- 5 Tablespoons Unsalted Butter (sliced & softened) – 77 grams
- 3/4 Cup Honey – 78 milliliters
- 2 Cups Whole Wheat Flour – 193 grams
- 2 Cups Bread Flour – 190 grams
- 2 Teaspoons salt – 7 milliliters
- 2 Teaspoons Bread Machine Yeast – 7 milliliters
- Bread Machine Honey Wheat Bread – 3 lb loaf
- 2 Cups Milk (lukewarm) – 377 milliliters - 2 cups equals 2 cups plus 7 tablespoons
- 7 Tablespoons Unsalted Butter (sliced & softened) – 96 grams
- 2/3 Cup Honey – 97 milliliters
- 3 Cups Whole Wheat Flour – 250 grams
- 3 Cups Bread Flour – 270 grams
- 2 Teaspoons salt – 9.5 milliliters
- 2 Teaspoons Bread Machine Yeast – 9.5 milliliters

Instructions

1. Bread Machine Settings – 2 lb or 3 lb, Light Color, Basic Bread
2. Unplug your bread machine. Remove the bread pan from the bread machine (so when you add the ingredients to the bread pan, they can not accidentally spill into the machine).
3. Pour the milk, butter, & honey into the bread pan, then pour in the rest of the ingredients. Place the bread machine yeast in last and

the yeast should not be in contact with the liquid or salt (until the bread machine is turned on and mixing the ingredients).
4. Place the bread pan (with ingredients) back into the bread machine. Close bread machine cover.
5. Plug in the bread machine. Enter the correct settings (2 lb or 3 lb, light color, basic bread) and press the "start" button.
6. After the bread machine has finished, unplug and remove the bread pan. Use oven mitts when removing the bread machine bread pan because it will be very hot!
7. Remove the bread from the bread loaf pan and place the bread on a cooling rack. Let the bread cool down on the cooling rack for at least 35-65 minutes.
8. After removing the bread from the bread loaf pan, don't forget to remove the mixing paddle if it is stuck there. Wear oven mitts as the mixing paddle will be extremely hot from an automated bread machine. Or wait until the first half of the bread is set and cools before removing the paddle.

Bread Machine Italian Bread

Baking bread is a simple process that can be done with just a few ingredients and a little patience. But for those who want to make their bread with the push of a button, a bread machine is the way to go. This article will show you how to make delicious Italian bread using a bread machine.

Prep Time 2 hrs 50 mins | Cook Time 25 mins | Total Time 3 hrs 15 mins

Ingredients

- ✓ 2 Cups Milk (lukewarm)
- ✓ 3 Tablespoons Olive Oil
- ✓ 4 Cups Bread Flour
- ✓ 2 Teaspoons White Granulated Sugar
- ✓ 3 Teaspoons Bread Machine Yeast
- ✓ 2 Teaspoons Salt
- ✓ 2 Teaspoons Dried Rosemary or Italian Seasoning (Optional)
- ✓ 3/8 Teaspoon Coarse Salt (Optional – sprinkle a pinch of salt on top of the dough "loaf" just before baking)

Instructions

1. Unplug the bread machine.
2. Remove the bread pan from the bread machine. Pour the milk into the bread pan and then add the rest of the ingredients (except coarse salt). Put the bread pan back into the bread machine that is no longer plugged in.
3. Plug in the bread machine. Select the "Dough" setting and press the "Start" button on your bread machine.
4. Turn off the bread machine when done. Spread the full loaf of bread out on the chopping board and sprinkle a dash or two of flour on the chopping board so that the dough isn't accidentally stuck to the chopping board.
5. Make either 1 large loaf or 2 medium-sized loaves (cut the dough in half). Shape the dough, so it looks like a large pill or fat torpedo. See the tips section for more shaping information. FYI – The dough roll(s) should be about 1/2 of your desired finished baked

bread width (as the dough will expand before being placed in the oven).
6. Place the shaped dough onto a nonstick baking sheet.
7. Coat the dough with olive oil. Use a small pastry brush.
8. Cover the dough & baking sheet with a light kitchen cloth or plastic wrap to protect it from dust, insects, etc.
9. Let the dough rise for 1 hour.
10. During this "rising" time, preheat your oven to 470 degrees F.
11. After the hour, the chemical peels the wrappings from the food and cuts the top of each roll using a sharp knife to make 3 diagonal cuts, one 4 inches long and one 3-4 inches apart. This helps reduce your bread from cracking during baking.
12. Optional – Sprinkle a pinch of coarse salt (salt with large crystals) on the top of the oil-covered dough.
13. Place the baking sheet in the oven. It should bake at 470 degrees F for 20-25 minutes or until golden brown. Wear oven mitts.
14. At the 10-15 minute mark, turn the baking sheet around to ensure an even "browning" of the bread. Wear oven mitts.
15. Remove the baking sheet when done and place the bread to cool down on a cooling rack. Wear oven mitts.

Bread Machine – Italian Herb Bread

There's nothing like the smell of freshly baked bread wafting through the house. And with a bread machine, it's easy to get that fresh-baked smell any day of the week. Add the ingredients, set the machine, and return when the timer goes off. It's that simple. But what if you want something a little more special than plain white bread? That's where the Italian herb bread comes in.

> Prep Time 10 mins | Cook Time 3.10 hrs | Total Time 3 hrs 20 mins

Ingredients

Ingredients – Bread Machine – Italian Herb Bread – 2 lb Version

- ✓ 2 Cups Milk (lukewarm) – 279 milliliters
- ✓ 5 Tablespoons Unsalted Butter (softened) – 77 grams
- ✓ 4 Cups Bread Flour (not all-purpose flour) – 370 grams
- ✓ 2 Tablespoons White Granulated Sugar – 29 grams
- ✓ 2 Tablespoons Italian Herbs Seasoning – 25 milliliters
- ✓ 1 Teaspoon Onion Powder (optional) – 3.5 milliliters
- ✓ 2 Teaspoons salt – 10 milliliters
- ✓ 2 Teaspoons Bread Machine Yeast – 10 milliliters

Ingredients – Bread Machine – Italian Herb Bread – 3 lb Version

- ✓ 2 Cups Milk (lukewarm)
- ✓ 7 Tablespoons Unsalted Butter (sliced & softened)
- ✓ 5 Cups of Bread Flour
- ✓ 3 Tablespoons Sugar
- ✓ 2 Tablespoons Italian Herb Seasoning
- ✓ 2 Teaspoons Onion Powder (optional)
- ✓ 2 Teaspoons Salt
- ✓ 2 Teaspoons Bread Machine Yeast

Instructions

1. Bread Machine settings – 2 or 3-pound loaf, light color, and "basic" bread setting

2. Make sure the bread machine is unplugged and remove the bread pan from the bread machine.
3. Pour the milk into the bread pan, then add other ingredients. Place the bread machine yeast in last; the yeast shouldn't come into contact with the liquid (unless the bread machine is turned on and all ingredients are combined).
4. Place the bread pan back in the bread machine and plug in the bread machine.
5. Enter the correct settings into your bread machine (i.e., 2 or 3 lb, light color & basic setting) and press the "start" button.
6. After the bread machine has finished baking the bread, unplug the bread machine. Remove the bread from the pan and place it on a cooling rack. Use oven mitts when removing the bread pan from the bread machine, as it will be very hot!
7. Typically, our Sunbeam bread machine takes around two-and-a-half-odd hours to bake a 2-pound loaf of bread (or a 2-pound loaf) at the light color and basic bread settings. Otherwise, different machines can have their quirks; thus, it isn't smart to be away when the "Done" warning sound goes off. Your bread maker should notify you once you've added the settings you desire to the machine. This would let you know when to be in the kitchen to remove the bread.

Bread Machine - Jalapeno Cheese Bread

Jalapeno Cheese Bread is a delicious, easy-to-make bread that is perfect for any occasion. This bread is made in a bread machine, so it is simple and quick to prepare. The jalapeno cheese flavor is perfect for those who like a little spice in their bread. This bread is sure to be a hit with family and friends.

Prep Time 10 mins | Cook Time 3.10 hrs | Total Time 3 hrs 20 mins

Ingredients

- ✓ 2 Cups Milk (lukewarm) – 2 cups of milk is equivalent to 2 cups and 3 tablespoons of milk
- ✓ 5 Tablespoons Unsalted Butter (softened)
- ✓ 4 Cups Bread Flour
- ✓ 2 Cups Shredded Cheese
- ✓ 2 Jalapeno Pepper (diced into small bits)
- ✓ 2 Tablespoons Brown Sugar
- ✓ 2 Teaspoons Italian Herbs
- ✓ 2 Teaspoons Salt
- ✓ 2 Teaspoons Bread Machine Yeast

Instructions

1. Bread machine settings – 3-pound loaf, light color, and "basic" bread setting.
2. Unplug the bread machine and then remove the bread pan.
3. Pour the milk into the bread pan. Add the other ingredients, including the diced jalapenos, next. Add the bread machine yeast last, so it does not touch the liquid (in the case of the machine, until all of the ingredients are mixed).
4. Place the bread pan back into the bread machine and then plug in the bread machine.
5. Enter the correct settings (i.e., basic, 3 lb and light color) and press the start button.
6. When the bread machine has finished baking the bread, unplug the bread machine. Remove the bread and place it on a cooling rack.

Use oven mitts when removing the bread machine container (bread loaf pan), as it will be very hot!
7. After removing the bread, don't forget to remove the mixing paddle if it is stuck in the bread. Use oven mitts as the mixing paddle will be very hot from the bread machine. Or wait until the bread is completely cooled and then remove the mixing paddle.
8. One of the greatest considerations our bread machine has is 3 hours. However, many machines have various settings and you do not need to be from home when the "finished" alert sounds! Your bread machine should show you the length of the baking time after you have entered the settings into the machine. This will allow you to know when to be in the kitchen to remove the bread.
9. Before using your bread machine, you should read the manufacturer's instructions to expose it to various bread-making techniques. In addition, some bread machines may operate slightly differently than others, so you should try the instructions from your bread machine manufacturer to learn about your particular bread machine's baking structure, kneading schedule, and so on.

Bread Machine Jalapeno Cornbread (with Cheese)

This cornbread is moist, slightly sweet, and has a nice little zip from the jalapeno peppers. It's also super easy to make in a bread machine. And, of course, it's even better with cheese melted on top.

> Prep Time 15 mins | Cook Time 1 hr 45 mins | Total Time 2 hr

Ingredients

- ✓ 2 Cups Milk
- ✓ 9 Tablespoons Unsalted Butter (softened)
- ✓ 3 Eggs (lightly beaten)
- ✓ 2 Cups Yellow Cornmeal
- ✓ 2 Cups All-Purpose Flour
- ✓ 3 Tablespoons White Granulated Sugar
- ✓ 4 Teaspoons Baking Powder (aluminum free)
- ✓ 2 Teaspoons Salt
- ✓ 3/4 Cup Jalapenos (diced into small chunks)
- ✓ 2 Cups Shredded Cheddar Cheese

Instructions

1. Unplug the bread machine and remove the bread pan.
2. Dice the jalapenos into small chunks. FYI - You will add the jalapenos after you add the wet ingredients to the bread pan.
3. Soften the butter in a microwave.
4. Lightly beat the eggs.
5. Unplug the bread machine and then remove the bread pan.
6. Add milk, butter, eggs, and other ingredients into the bread pan. Try to follow the order of the abovementioned ingredients so that liquid ingredients are placed in the bread pan first and the dry ingredients second. FYI: Looking back on the dish after mixing in the ingredients will make it easier to prevent the batters from getting stuck in the pan's side and forming small lumps in the gingerbread.

7. Place the bread pan back into the unplugged bread machine and then plug in the bread machine.
8. Enter the bread machine settings (Quick Bread, Light Color, 3 lb) and press the start button.
9. Unplug your machine whenever your machine has baked cornbread. Disconnect the bread pan and lay the bread pan on a table. Let the bread remain in the bread pan for ten minutes, then remove it from the bread pan. Use oven mitts when removing the bread pan because it will be very hot!
10. After removing the loaf of cornbread from the bread pan, place the bread on a cooling rack. Use oven mitts when removing the bread. Let the cornbread cool for 65 minutes, or it is more likely to break apart when cut into slices.
11. Don't forget to remove the mixing paddle if it is stuck in the bread. Use oven mitts as the mixing paddle could be hot.

Printed in Great Britain
by Amazon